EVery DAy Matters 2026 Diary

A Year of Inspiration for the Mind, Body and Spirit

Created by

Jess Sharp

as seen on Instagram
@jessrachelsharp

WATKINS
Sharing Wisdom
Since 1893

Every Day Matters 2026 Diary

First published in UK and USA in 2025 by
Watkins, an imprint of Watkins Media Limited
Unit 11, Shepperton House
89–93 Shepperton Road
London N1 3DF

enquiries@watkinspublishing.com

Designed by Watkins Media Limited

Publisher: Fiona Robertson
Commissioning Editor: Brittany Willis
Illustrator and Author: Jess Sharp
Head of Design: Karen Smith
Designer: Sneha Alexander
Production: Uzma Taj

ISBN: 978-178678-961-7

Printed in China

Signs of the Zodiac 2026:

≈ Aquarius	January 20–February 17
♓ Pisces	February 18–March 19
♈ Aries	March 20–April 19
♉ Taurus	April 20–May 20
♊ Gemini	May 21–June 20
♋ Cancer	June 21–July 21
♌ Leo	July 22–August 22
♍ Virgo	August 23–September 22
♎ Libra	September 23–October 22
♏ Scorpio	October 23–November 21
♐ Sagittarius	November 22–December 20
♑ Capricorn	December 21–January 19, 2027

Phases of the Moon:

- ● New moon
- ☽ First quarter
- ○ Full moon
- ☾ Last quarter

Abbreviations:

BCE: Before Common Era (equivalent of BC)
CE: Common Era (equivalent of AD)
UK: United Kingdom
SCO: Scotland
NIR: Northern Ireland
ROI: Republic of Ireland
CAN: Canada
USA: United States of America
NZ: New Zealand
AUS: Australia
ACT: Australian Capital Territory
NSW: New South Wales
NT: Northern Territory
QLD: Queensland
SA: South Australia
TAS: Tasmania
VIC: Victoria
WA: Western Australia

Publisher's Notes:

All dates relating to the zodiac signs and the
phases of the moon are based on Greenwich Mean
Time (GMT).

All North American holiday dates are based
on Eastern Standard Time (EST).

Islamic holidays may vary by a day or two.

Dates were correct at the time of going to press.

The manufacturer's authorised representative
in the EU for product safety is: eucomply
OÜ - Pärnu mnt 139b-14, 11317 Tallinn,
Estonia, hello@eucompliancepartner.com,
www.eucompliancepartner.com

2025

JANUARY
M TU W TH F SA SU
          1 2 3 4 5
6 7 8 9 10 11 12
13 14 15 16 17 18 19
20 21 22 23 24 25 26
27 28 29 30 31

FEBRUARY
M TU W TH F SA SU
                1 2
3 4 5 6 7 8 9
10 11 12 13 14 15 16
17 18 19 20 21 22 23
24 25 26 27 28

MARCH
M TU W TH F SA SU
                1 2
3 4 5 6 7 8 9
10 11 12 13 14 15 16
17 18 19 20 21 22 23
24 25 26 27 28 29 30
31

APRIL
M TU W TH F SA SU
1 2 3 4 5 6
7 8 9 10 11 12 13
14 15 16 17 18 19 20
21 22 23 24 25 26 27
28 29 30

MAY
M TU W TH F SA SU
            1 2 3 4
5 6 7 8 9 10 11
12 13 14 15 16 17 18
19 20 21 22 23 24 25
26 27 28 29 30 31

JUNE
M TU W TH F SA SU
                     1
2 3 4 5 6 7 8
9 10 11 12 13 14 15
16 17 18 19 20 21 22
23 24 25 26 27 28 29
30

JULY
M TU W TH F SA SU
      1 2 3 4 5 6
7 8 9 10 11 12 13
14 15 16 17 18 19 20
21 22 23 24 25 26 27
28 29 30 31

AUGUST
M TU W TH F SA SU
                1 2 3
4 5 6 7 8 9 10
11 12 13 14 15 16 17
18 19 20 21 22 23 24
25 26 27 28 29 30 31

SEPTEMBER
M TU W TH F SA SU
1 2 3 4 5 6 7
8 9 10 11 12 13 14
15 16 17 18 19 20 21
22 23 24 25 26 27 28
29 30

OCTOBER
M TU W TH F SA SU
          1 2 3 4 5
6 7 8 9 10 11 12
13 14 15 16 17 18 19
20 21 22 23 24 25 26
27 28 29 30 31

NOVEMBER
M TU W TH F SA SU
                1 2
3 4 5 6 7 8 9
10 11 12 13 14 15 16
17 18 19 20 21 22 23
24 25 26 27 28 29 30

DECEMBER
M TU W TH F SA SU
1 2 3 4 5 6 7
8 9 10 11 12 13 14
15 16 17 18 19 20 21
22 23 24 25 26 27 28
29 30 31

2026

JANUARY
M TU W TH F SA SU
            1 2 3 4
5 6 7 8 9 10 11
12 13 14 15 16 17 18
19 20 21 22 23 24 25
26 27 28 29 30 31

FEBRUARY
M TU W TH F SA SU
                     1
2 3 4 5 6 7 8
9 10 11 12 13 14 15
16 17 18 19 20 21 22
23 24 25 26 27 28

MARCH
M TU W TH F SA SU
                     1
2 3 4 5 6 7 8
9 10 11 12 13 14 15
16 17 18 19 20 21 22
23 24 25 26 27 28 29
30 31

APRIL
M TU W TH F SA SU
          1 2 3 4 5
6 7 8 9 10 11 12
13 14 15 16 17 18 19
20 21 22 23 24 25 26
27 28 29 30

MAY
M TU W TH F SA SU
                1 2 3
4 5 6 7 8 9 10
11 12 13 14 15 16 17
18 19 20 21 22 23 24
25 26 27 28 29 30 31

JUNE
M TU W TH F SA SU
1 2 3 4 5 6 7
8 9 10 11 12 13 14
15 16 17 18 19 20 21
22 23 24 25 26 27 28
29 30

JULY
M TU W TH F SA SU
          1 2 3 4 5
6 7 8 9 10 11 12
13 14 15 16 17 18 19
20 21 22 23 24 25 26
27 28 29 30 31

AUGUST
M TU W TH F SA SU
                1 2
3 4 5 6 7 8 9
10 11 12 13 14 15 16
17 18 19 20 21 22 23
24 25 26 27 28 29 30
31

SEPTEMBER
M TU W TH F SA SU
      1 2 3 4 5 6
7 8 9 10 11 12 13
14 15 16 17 18 19 20
21 22 23 24 25 26 27
28 29 30

OCTOBER
M TU W TH F SA SU
                1 2 3 4
5 6 7 8 9 10 11
12 13 14 15 16 17 18
19 20 21 22 23 24 25
26 27 28 29 30 31

NOVEMBER
M TU W TH F SA SU
                     1
2 3 4 5 6 7 8
9 10 11 12 13 14 15
16 17 18 19 20 21 22
23 24 25 26 27 28 29
30

DECEMBER
M TU W TH F SA SU
      1 2 3 4 5 6
7 8 9 10 11 12 13
14 15 16 17 18 19 20
21 22 23 24 25 26 27
28 29 30 31

2027

JANUARY
M TU W TH F SA SU
                1 2 3
4 5 6 7 8 9 10
11 12 13 14 15 16 17
18 19 20 21 22 23 24
25 26 27 28 29 30 31

FEBRUARY
M TU W TH F SA SU
1 2 3 4 5 6 7
8 9 10 11 12 13 14
15 16 17 18 19 20 21
22 23 24 25 26 27 28

MARCH
M TU W TH F SA SU
1 2 3 4 5 6 7
8 9 10 11 12 13 14
15 16 17 18 19 20 21
22 23 24 25 26 27 28
29 30 31

APRIL
M TU W TH F SA SU
            1 2 3 4
5 6 7 8 9 10 11
12 13 14 15 16 17 18
19 20 21 22 23 24 25
26 27 28 29 30

MAY
M TU W TH F SA SU
                  1 2
3 4 5 6 7 8 9
10 11 12 13 14 15 16
17 18 19 20 21 22 23
24 25 26 27 28 29 30
31

JUNE
M TU W TH F SA SU
      1 2 3 4 5 6
7 8 9 10 11 12 13
14 15 16 17 18 19 20
21 22 23 24 25 26 27
28 29 30

JULY
M TU W TH F SA SU
            1 2 3 4
5 6 7 8 9 10 11
12 13 14 15 16 17 18
19 20 21 22 23 24 25
26 27 28 29 30 31

AUGUST
M TU W TH F SA SU
                     1
2 3 4 5 6 7 8
9 10 11 12 13 14 15
16 17 18 19 20 21 22
23 24 25 26 27 28 29
30 31

SEPTEMBER
M TU W TH F SA SU
            1 2 3 4 5
6 7 8 9 10 11 12
13 14 15 16 17 18 19
20 21 22 23 24 25 26
27 28 29 30

OCTOBER
M TU W TH F SA SU
                1 2 3
4 5 6 7 8 9 10
11 12 13 14 15 16 17
18 19 20 21 22 23 24
25 26 27 28 29 30 31

NOVEMBER
M TU W TH F SA SU
1 2 3 4 5 6 7
8 9 10 11 12 13 14
15 16 17 18 19 20 21
22 23 24 25 26 27 28
29 30

DECEMBER
M TU W TH F SA SU
            1 2 3 4 5
6 7 8 9 10 11 12
13 14 15 16 17 18 19
20 21 22 23 24 25 26
27 28 29 30 31

2026 International Public Holidays

Argentina	Jan 1, Feb 16, Feb 17, Mar 24, Apr 2, Apr 3, May 1, May 25, Jun 17, Jun 20, Jul 9, Aug 17, Oct 12, Nov 23, Dec 8, Dec 25
Australia	Jan 1, Jan 26, Mar 2 (WA), Mar 9 (TAS, VIC, ACT), Apr 3, Apr 4 (exc TAS, WA), Apr 5 (exc SA, TAS), Apr 6, Apr 25, Apr 27 (ACT, WA), May 4 (NT, QLD), Jun 1 (WA, ACT), Jun 8 (exc QLD, WA), Sep 28 (WA), Oct 5 (ACT, NSW, SA), Dec 24 (NT, QLD, SA), Dec 25, Dec 26, Dec 28, Dec 31 (NT, SA)
Austria	Jan 1, Jan 6, Apr 6, May 1, May 14, May 25, Jun 4, Aug 15, Oct 26, Nov 1, Dec 8, Dec 25, Dec 26
Belgium	Jan 1, Apr 6, May 1, May 14, May 25, Jul 21, Aug 15, Nov 1, Nov 11, Dec 25
Brazil	Jan 1, Feb 16-17, Apr 3, Apr 21, May 1, Jun 4, Sep 7, Oct 12, Nov 2, Nov 15, Nov 20, Dec 25
Canada	Jan 1, Apr 5, Apr 6 (AB, NT, NU, QC), May 18 (exc NS, PEI), Jul 1, Sep 30 (AB, BC, MB, NL, PEI, YT), Oct 12 (exc NS, PEI), Nov 11 (exc MB, NS, ON, QC), Dec 25, Dec 26 (AB, NB, NL, NT, NU, ON)
China	Jan 1-2, Feb 16-22, Apr 5-6, May 1, Jun 19, Sep 25, Oct 1-7
Denmark	Jan 1, Apr 2-3, Apr 5-6, May 14, May 24-25, Dec 25-26
Finland	Jan 1, Jan 6, Apr 3, Apr 5-6, May 1, May 14, May 24, Jun 19-20, Oct 31, Dec 6, Dec 24-26
France	Jan 1, Apr 3, Apr 6, May 1, May 8, May 14, May 24-25, Jul 14, Aug 15, Nov 1, Nov 11, Dec 25-26
Germany	Jan 1, Apr 3, Apr 6, May 1, May 14, May 25, Oct 3, Dec 25-26
Greece	Jan 1, Jan 6, Feb 23, Mar 25, Apr 10, Apr 12-13, May 1, May 31, Jun 1, Aug 15, Oct 28, Dec 25-26
India	Jan 1, Jan 26, Feb 15, Mar 3, Mar 20-21, Mar 27, Mar 31, Apr 3, Apr 14, May 1, May 27, Jun 26, Aug 15, Aug 25, Sep 4, Oct 2, Oct 21, Nov 8, Nov 24, Dec 25
Indonesia	Jan 1, Jan 16, Feb 17, Mar 19-21, Apr 3, May 1, May 14, May 27, May 31, Jun 1, Jun 17, Aug 17, Aug 25, Dec 25
Israel	2 Apr, 8 Apr, Apr 22, May 22, Sep 12-13, Sep 21, Sep 26, Oct 3
Italy	Jan 1, Jan 6, Apr 5-6, Apr 25, May 1, Jun 2, Aug 15, Nov 1, Dec 8, Dec 25-26

Japan	Jan 1, Jan 12, Feb 11, Feb 23, Mar 20, Apr 29, May 3-5, Jul 20, Aug 11, Sep 21, Sep 23, Oct 12, Nov 3, Nov 23
Luxembourg	Jan 1, Apr 6, May 1, May 9, May 14, May 25, Jun 23, Aug 15, Nov 1, Dec 25-26
Mexico	Jan 1, Feb 2, Mar 16, Apr 2-3, May 1, May 5, Sep 16, Oct 12, Nov 2, Nov 16, Dec 12, Dec 25
Netherlands	Jan 1, Apr 3, Apr 5-6, Apr 27, May 5, May 14, May 24-25, Dec 25-26
New Zealand	Jan 1-2, Jan 19, Jan 26, Feb 2, Feb 6, Mar 9, Mar 23, Apr 3, Apr 6-7, Apr 25, Apr 27, Jun 1, Jul 10, Sep 28, Oct 23, Oct 26, Nov 2, Nov 13, Nov 30, Dec 25-26, Dec 28
Nigeria	Jan 1, Mar 20-21, Apr 3, Apr 6, May 1, May 27-28, Jun 12, Aug 25, Oct 1, Dec 25-26
Pakistan	Feb 5, Mar 21-23, Apr 6, May 1, May 27-28, Jun 25-26, Aug 14, Aug 25, Dec 25-26
Poland	Jan 1, Jan 6, Apr 5-6, May 1, May 3, May 24, Jun 4, Aug 15, Nov 1, Nov 11, Dec 25-26
Portugal	Jan 1, Apr 3, Apr 5, Apr 25, May 1, Jun 4, Jun 10, Aug 15, Oct 5, Nov 1, Dec 1, Dec 8, Dec 25
Republic of Ireland	Jan 1, Feb 2, Mar 17, Apr 6, May 4, Jun 1, Aug 3, Oct 26, Dec 25-26
Russia	Jan 1-8, Feb 23, Mar 8-9, May 1, May 9, May 11, Jun 12, Nov 4
South Africa	Jan 1, Mar 21, Apr 3, Apr 6, Apr 27, May 1, Jun 16, Aug 9-10, Sep 24, Dec 16, Dec 25-26
Spain	Jan 1, Jan 6, Apr 2 (exc Catalonia, Valencia), Apr 3, May 1, Aug 15, Oct 12, Nov 1, Dec 6, Dec 8 (exc Ceuta), Dec 25
Sweden	Jan 1, Jan 6, Apr 3, Apr 5-6, May 1, May 14, May 24, Jun 6, Jun 20, Oct 31, Dec 25-26
Turkey	Jan 1, Mar 20-22, Apr 23, May 1, May 19, May 27-30, Jul 15, Aug 30, Oct 29
United Kingdom	Jan 1, Jan 2 (SCO), Mar 17 (NI), Apr 3, Apr 6 (exc SCO), May 4, May 25, Jul 12-13 (NI), Aug 3 (SCO), Aug 31 (exc SCO), Nov 30 (SCO), Dec 25-26, Dec 28
United States	Jan 1, Jan 19, Feb 16, May 25, Jun 19, Jul 3-4, Sep 7, Oct 12, Nov 11, Nov 26, Dec 25

All information taken from publicholidays.com or timeanddate.com (US only).

WELCOME TO 2026!

Hello and welcome to 2026! There's a whole new exciting year stretching out before you. Whatever's happened during the last 12 months, you deserve to stand at the start of this year with a proud heart. You made it through, even when you felt like you couldn't. I hope you can see that for the amazing achievement it is and offer yourself the grace and compassion you deserve for navigating all those tricky twists and turns.

This diary focuses on a positive theme each month, and this year they include Intention, Self-Worth, Happiness, Stillness, Restoration, Dreams, Connection, Empowerment, Self-Soothing, Balance, Adaptability and Reminiscence. Within each month, you'll find inspiring weekly quotes and prompts to support you in getting the most from 2026, along with plenty of space to organize your weeks.

I hope that this diary will help you embrace all that the coming months have to offer and gently guide you in some personal reflection. So here's to 2026 – may it be a year full of gorgeous opportunities and wondrous things!

JANUARY

INTENTION

Welcome, January! What a perfect month to start setting our intentions for how we'd like this year to feel and what we'd like to concentrate on. Much like a moth seeks light in the darkness, we should be striving to find our light, too. How do you see this year ideally working out? What would you like it to be filled with? It's all too easy to get swept up in what the world thinks we need or should be doing and feeling, and to chase the aspirations that others set for us, but this can leave us feeling empty and run down.

Sometimes, when we hone in on what's meaningful to us, what makes us feel fulfilled and where we find true enjoyment, it's easier to work out what we really do need to do in order to achieve a happier and more well-rounded life. Whether it's taking steps to follow your dreams, allocating more time to yourself or your family or pursuing a new career, let this be the year you live with more intention.

AFFIRMATION OF THE MONTH

I choose myself; everything is possible for me

DEC 29 – JAN 4
INTENTION

29 / MONDAY

30 / TUESDAY

31 / WEDNESDAY
New Year's Eve

THREE POSITIVE THINGS THIS WEEK

1
2
3

"The future depends on what you do today."

MAHATMA GANDHI (1869–1948), ACTIVIST AND LEADER

1 / THURSDAY
New Year's Day
Kwanzaa ends

_____

_____

_____

_____

_____

_____

_____

_____

_____

2 / FRIDAY
Public Holiday (SCO)

_____

_____

_____

_____

_____

_____

_____

_____

_____

3 / SATURDAY ○

_____

_____

_____

_____

4 / SUNDAY

_____

_____

_____

_____

_____

LOOK TO THE PRESENT

To know what we'd like to see more of in our future, we first have to look at where we are right now. Take a moment to think about all the things that you love in your life. Then turn to the Inspired Journalling section at the back of this diary and make a list of them. You can refer back to this list throughout the year.

JAN 5 – JAN 11

INTENTION

5 / MONDAY
Twelfth Night

6 / TUESDAY
Epiphany

7 / WEDNESDAY
Christmas Day (Orthodox)

THREE POSITIVE THINGS THIS WEEK

1
2
3

> ## "The best way to predict the future is to create it."

ABRAHAM LINCOLN (1809–1865), US PRESIDENT

8 / THURSDAY

9 / FRIDAY

10 / SATURDAY ☾

11 / SUNDAY

VISUALIZE THE FUTURE

When you think of your ideal vision for the coming year, what do you see? What's important to you? Knowing what it is we'd like to change allows us to make the necessary arrangements to do just that. This week, think about how you could make some small changes to put this vision of yours into action.

12 / MONDAY

13 / TUESDAY

14 / WEDNESDAY
New Year's Day (Orthodox)

THREE POSITIVE THINGS THIS WEEK

1
2
3

15 / THURSDAY

16 / FRIDAY

17 / SATURDAY

18 / SUNDAY ●

THINK ABOUT THE PEOPLE AND PLACES YOU LOVE

We all have friends, family members and places that mean the world to us. The people and places who are always there when we need them and who make us feel loved and validated. Who and what are they for you? Can you make some plans to see or visit them this year?

JAN 19 – JAN 25
INTENTION

19 / MONDAY
Martin Luther King Jr Day

20 / TUESDAY ≈
Inauguration Day (USA)

21 / WEDNESDAY

THREE POSITIVE THINGS THIS WEEK

1 _____

2 _____

3 _____

"Be happy. It's one way of being wise."

COLETTE (1873–1954), AUTHOR

22 / THURSDAY

23 / FRIDAY

24 / SATURDAY

25 / SUNDAY
Burns Night (SCO)

DESCRIBE YOUR PERFECT DAY

What would your perfect day look like? This week, sit and write a little timeline of that perfect day, step by step. Who are you with? What would you do? By being able to clarify exactly what your most fulfilling and happy day looks like, you'll be better placed to implement it and make it a reality throughout 2026.

JANUARY OVERVIEW

M	TU	W	TH	F	SA	SU
29	30	31	1	2	3	4
5	6	7	8	9	10	11
12	13	14	15	16	17	18
19	20	21	22	23	24	25
26	27	28	29	30	31	1

This month I am grateful for . . .

REFLECTIONS ON INTENTION

In what ways have you brought more intention into your life this month?

_____

_____

_____

_____

How has it felt to think about how your life currently looks and feels, and how you'd like it to look and feel?

_____

_____

_____

_____

Draw a heart. Inside, draw all your feelings, giving more space to the more prominent ones. What would you like to see more of? And what's taking up too much room? Can you use this insight to set your intentions for the year ahead?

FEBRUARY

SELF-WORTH

How do you feel about yourself? Do you find it hard to think of yourself kindly and to give yourself the compliments and credit you deserve? Recognizing our own worth and potential can be a difficult thing to do, especially when we have low self-esteem or have been told the opposite throughout our lives. Our internal voices can sometimes be incredibly cruel and relentless, and may cloud our judgement with repeated negative scripts that aren't true or helpful. It can be hard not to listen or let this affect us.

The more we love ourselves, the more we recognize our potential, and the more we stop believing that we have to play small and downplay our brilliance, the more fearsome and unstoppable we become. So this is the month to start recognizing just how wonderful you are. This is the month to be gentler and kinder to yourself. This month, put it all into practice and see where it can take you ...

AFFIRMATION OF THE MONTH

My self-worth grows when I praise myself

JAN 26 – FEB 1
SELF-WORTH

26 / MONDAY ☽
Australia Day

27 / TUESDAY
International Holocaust
Remembrance Day

28 / WEDNESDAY

THREE POSITIVE THINGS THIS WEEK

1

2

3

> "You yourself, as much as anybody in the entire universe, deserve your love and affection."

BUDDHA (c.563–483 BCE), SPIRITUAL MASTER

29 / THURSDAY

30 / FRIDAY

31 / SATURDAY

1 / SUNDAY ○
St Brigid's Day (Imbolc)
Black History Month begins
(USA, CAN)

BE KIND TO YOURSELF

When our internal voice is mean and bullying, this can really affect our feelings of self-worth. This week, be aware of whether you're kind and positive about yourself or not. Every time you find yourself being mean or negative, gently stop yourself. If you wouldn't say it to a friend, you shouldn't be saying it to yourself.

FEB 2 – FEB 8
SELF-WORTH

2 / MONDAY
Groundhog Day
Candlemas

3 / TUESDAY

4 / WEDNESDAY

THREE POSITIVE THINGS THIS WEEK

1
2
3

> ## "Let us be grateful to people who make us happy, they are the charming gardeners who make our souls blossom."
>
> MARCEL PROUST (1871–1922), WRITER AND CRITIC

5 / THURSDAY

6 / FRIDAY
Waitangi Day

7 / SATURDAY

8 / SUNDAY

FIND YOUR PEOPLE

When we're surrounded by people who always see the negatives, who don't support us or who make us feel worse about ourselves, it's hard to channel self-worth. Think about who these people might be for you and quietly distance yourself from them. Instead, find people who will help you flourish and grow into your best self.

FEB 9 – FEB 15
SELF-WORTH

9 / MONDAY ☾

10 / TUESDAY

11 / WEDNESDAY

THREE POSITIVE THINGS THIS WEEK

1
2
3

> ## "To love oneself is the beginning of a lifelong romance."
>
> OSCAR WILDE (1854–1900), POET AND PLAYWRIGHT

12 / THURSDAY
Abraham Lincoln's birthday

_____

_____

_____

_____

_____

_____

13 / FRIDAY

_____

_____

_____

_____

_____

_____

14 / SATURDAY
St Valentine's Day

_____

_____

_____

15 / SUNDAY
Nirvana Day
Maha Shivaratri

_____

_____

_____

_____

_____

_____

WHAT DO YOU LIKE ABOUT YOURSELF?

We can often be our own worst critics. This week, turn to the Inspired Journalling section at the back of this diary and make a list of everything you love about yourself and all the things you've done that you're proud of. Refer back to this list if you ever need a pick-me-up – let these words soothe you.

FEB 16 – FEB 22
SELF-WORTH

16 / MONDAY
Presidents' Day

_____

_____

_____

_____

_____

_____

_____

_____

_____

_____

_____

17 / TUESDAY ⬤
Chinese New Year
Ramadan begins at sundown
Shrove Tuesday

_____

_____

_____

_____

_____

_____

_____

_____

_____

_____

_____

18 / WEDNESDAY ♓
Ash Wednesday

_____

_____

_____

_____

_____

_____

_____

_____

_____

_____

_____

THREE POSITIVE THINGS THIS WEEK

1 _____

2 _____

3 _____

> ## "Fall in love with yourself, with life, and then with whoever you want."
>
> FRIDA KAHLO (1907–1954), ARTIST

19 / THURSDAY

---

20 / FRIDAY

---

21 / SATURDAY

---

22 / SUNDAY

SAY "I LOVE ME"

It's hard to even whisper these words, isn't it? Yet focusing on what you love about yourself can really help strengthen your sense of self-worth. Pick three things from the list you made last week, look at yourself in the mirror and tell yourself "I love me because ..." The more you say it, the more you'll start to believe it.

FEBRUARY OVERVIEW

M	TU	W	TH	F	SA	SU
26	27	28	29	30	31	1
2	3	4	5	6	7	8
9	10	11	12	13	14	15
16	17	18	19	20	21	22
23	24	25	26	27	28	1

This month I am grateful for . . .

_____

_____

_____

_____

_____

_____

_____

_____

REFLECTIONS ON SELF-WORTH

How have you found concentrating on your self-worth this month?

_____

_____

_____

_____

_____

Are there any areas of your life that you think might benefit if you had a better sense of self-worth?

_____

_____

_____

_____

_____

Find a picture of yourself as a child doing something you loved. Write down all the compliments you'd tell this little person about how wonderful and talented they are. Keep this to remind yourself how wonderful and talented you've always been.

_____

_____

_____

_____

_____

MARCH

HAPPINESS

Happiness can often feel elusive. Many of us treat it like a final destination that we'll one day reach – just as soon as we've ticked off our to-do list and all the other obstacles are out of the way. The problem with this mentality is that there will always be other things getting in the way and popping up when we least expect them. If we're waiting for them to be dealt with before we let in happiness, we'll be waiting forever.

Maybe it's time to embrace the happiness within the chaos. To open our arms to imperfection and find the joy nestling in it. Of course, happiness is never a constant. But if we can recognize and welcome it when it appears, that's got to make life a little bit sweeter, hasn't it? Use the prompts this month to explore what makes you happy and how you can embrace and welcome more happiness into your life.

AFFIRMATION OF THE MONTH

I open my heart to happiness and embrace the warmth it brings

FEB 23 – MAR 1

HAPPINESS

23 / MONDAY

24 / TUESDAY ☽

25 / WEDNESDAY

THREE POSITIVE THINGS THIS WEEK

1

2

3

> "Find ecstasy in life; the mere sense of living is joy enough."
>
> EMILY DICKINSON (1830–1886), POET

26 / THURSDAY

_____
_____
_____
_____
_____
_____
_____
_____
_____
_____

27 / FRIDAY

_____
_____
_____
_____
_____
_____
_____
_____
_____

28 / SATURDAY

_____
_____
_____
_____

1 / SUNDAY
St David's Day

_____
_____
_____
_____

WELCOME HAPPINESS IN YOUR LIFE

Happiness comes in many shapes and sizes, from the little things that simply make us smile to major, life-changing moments. Write down three things that have made you feel positive today. Revisit this list when you need reminders of the joys in your life. I've also included space in this diary for you to continue to do this weekly.

MAR 2 – MAR 8

HAPPINESS

2 / MONDAY
Labour Day (WA)
Purim begins at sundown

3 / TUESDAY ○

4 / WEDNESDAY
Holi (Festival of Colours)

THREE POSITIVE THINGS THIS WEEK

1

2

3

> "We don't laugh because we're happy
> – we're happy because we laugh."
>
> WILLIAM JAMES (1842–1910), PHILOSOPHER AND PSYCHOLOGIST

5 / THURSDAY
World Book Day

6 / FRIDAY

7 / SATURDAY

8 / SUNDAY
International Women's Day
Daylight Saving Time starts
(USA, CAN)

TAKE LAUGHTER AS A TONIC

Nothing beats a good belly laugh. Laughter connects us with others and eases stress. This week, try to seek out something that really tickles you, be it a phone call with a friend who makes you howl with laughter, a TV show or a few funny YouTube videos. Laughter is joyous and you can never have too much.

MAR 9 – MAR 15

HAPPINESS

9 / MONDAY
Commonwealth Day

10 / TUESDAY

11 / WEDNESDAY ☾

THREE POSITIVE THINGS THIS WEEK

1
2
3

> "Happiness is the settling of the soul into its most appropriate spot."
>
> ARISTOTLE (384–322 BCE), PHILOSOPHER

12 / THURSDAY

_____
_____
_____
_____
_____
_____
_____
_____
_____
_____
_____

13 / FRIDAY

_____
_____
_____
_____
_____
_____
_____
_____
_____
_____
_____

14 / SATURDAY

_____
_____
_____
_____

15 / SUNDAY
Mother's Day (UK)
Laylatul Qadr

_____
_____
_____
_____

WHEN WERE YOU HAPPIEST?

This week, think back over the past few months. When did you feel most happy? Why do you think that is? Was it because of a specific place, person or event? Try to implement or plan more of whatever made you feel this happiness so you can enjoy it again in the future. It's key to invite as much happiness into your life as you can!

MAR 16 – MAR 22
HAPPINESS

16 / MONDAY

17 / TUESDAY
St Patrick's Day

18 / WEDNESDAY
Ramadan ends at sundown

THREE POSITIVE THINGS THIS WEEK

1

2

3

> "There are two ways of spreading light: to be the candle or the mirror that reflects it."

EDITH WHARTON (1862–1937), WRITER AND DESIGNER

19 / THURSDAY ●
Eid al-Fitr begins at sundown

20 / FRIDAY ♈
Spring Equinox (UK, ROI, USA, CAN)

21 / SATURDAY
Autumn Equinox (AUS, NZ)

_____
_____
_____
_____
_____
_____
_____
_____
_____
_____

22 / SUNDAY

_____
_____
_____
_____
_____

SPREAD A LITTLE HAPPINESS

A small act of kindness or positivity can bring so much happiness to someone's day. This week, do something nice for someone, whether buying a coffee for a stranger or leaving a kind anonymous note on a public bench. It might seem insignificant to you, but to someone else it could be the lifeline that they need.

MAR 23 – MAR 29

HAPPINESS

23 / MONDAY

24 / TUESDAY

25 / WEDNESDAY ☽

THREE POSITIVE THINGS THIS WEEK

1
2
3

> "Happiness is a gift and the trick is not to expect it, but to delight in it when it comes."

CHARLES DICKENS (1812–1870), WRITER

26 / THURSDAY

_____
_____
_____
_____
_____
_____
_____
_____
_____
_____
_____

27 / FRIDAY

_____
_____
_____
_____
_____
_____
_____
_____
_____
_____
_____

28 / SATURDAY

_____
_____
_____
_____

29 / SUNDAY

Daylight Saving Time
starts (UK)
British Summer Time begins
Palm Sunday

_____
_____
_____
_____

WHAT MAKES ME HAPPY?

It's important to recognize what lights us up and makes us happy. This allows us to focus on what we really care about, so we can seek out these moments more often. This week, turn to the Inspired Journalling section at the back of this diary and make a list of all the things that make you happy. Revisit this whenever you need to.

MARCH OVERVIEW

M	TU	W	TH	F	SA	SU
23	24	25	26	27	28	1
2	3	4	5	6	7	8
9	10	11	12	13	14	15
16	17	18	19	20	21	22
23	24	25	26	27	28	29
30	31	1	2	3	4	5

This month I am grateful for . . .

_____

_____

_____

_____

_____

_____

REFLECTIONS ON HAPPINESS

How have you sought more happiness in your life this month?

_____

_____

_____

_____

How has it felt looking more clearly at what brings you happiness and implementing this?

_____

_____

_____

_____

Draw a simple tree with lots of leaves, and write down something that makes you happy on each leaf – anything or anyone that brings you joy. Refer back to this whenever you need a reminder of where your happiness lies.

APRIL

STILLNESS

The world we live in can be a very loud and busy place. We spend so much time dashing about, trying to tick off every little thing on our to-do lists, and we then often feel lazy when we do slow down. Even if we're not frantically rushing around, our lives and our minds can struggle under the burden of hectic modern life. With just about everyone having a digital device of some sort, life can seem incredibly overwhelming, with all that data adding to the sensory overload we already feel. Finding stillness in a world like ours is difficult, but it can be done, and the benefits include a really positive impact on both our minds and our bodies.

This month's prompts aim to help you find some calm and stillness within your busy daily life. Each week focuses on a different way to help you find serenity and take some much needed time away from the white noise of modern living, hopefully supporting your physical and mental wellbeing along the way.

AFFIRMATION OF THE MONTH

I breathe out stress and
breathe in stillness

MAR 30 – APR 5

STILLNESS

30 / MONDAY

_____
_____
_____
_____
_____
_____
_____
_____
_____
_____
_____
_____
_____

31 / TUESDAY

_____
_____
_____
_____
_____
_____
_____
_____
_____
_____
_____
_____
_____

1 / WEDNESDAY

April Fools' Day
Passover begins at sundown

_____
_____
_____
_____
_____
_____
_____
_____
_____
_____
_____
_____

THREE POSITIVE THINGS THIS WEEK

1 _____

2 _____

3 _____

> ## "The quieter you become, the more you are able to hear."
>
> RUMI (1207–1273), POET

2 / THURSDAY ○
Maundy Thursday

_____
_____
_____
_____
_____
_____
_____
_____
_____
_____

3 / FRIDAY
Good Friday

_____
_____
_____
_____
_____
_____
_____
_____
_____
_____

4 / SATURDAY
Easter Saturday

_____
_____
_____
_____

5 / SUNDAY
Easter Sunday

_____
_____
_____
_____
_____

GIVE LIFE YOUR FULL ATTENTION

Modern technology makes it easy for us to become overstimulated and overwhelmed. We watch TV while scrolling, we eat while checking our emails and we spend time with others while glued to our devices. This week, turn off distractions and spend some quality time with someone in stillness.

APR 6 – APR 12
STILLNESS

6 / MONDAY
Easter Monday

7 / TUESDAY

8 / WEDNESDAY

THREE POSITIVE THINGS THIS WEEK

1
2
3

> ## "Rivers know this: there is no hurry.
> ## We shall get there someday."

A A MILNE (1882–1956), WRITER

9 / THURSDAY
Passover ends at sundown

_____

_____

_____

_____

_____

_____

_____

_____

_____

_____

10 / FRIDAY ☽
Good Friday (Orthodox)

_____

_____

_____

_____

_____

_____

_____

_____

_____

_____

11 / SATURDAY
Easter Saturday (Orthodox)

_____

_____

_____

_____

12 / SUNDAY
Easter Sunday (Orthodox)

_____

_____

_____

_____

_____

TAKE A MINDFUL SHOWER

Focusing on the senses is a wonderful way of guiding our mind to the present and finding stillness. This week, when you shower, be really aware of your thoughts and feelings. Sense the water as it falls on your skin. Smell the soap. Savour each and every sensation, gently refocusing on these if your mind wanders.

APR 13 – APR 19
STILLNESS

13 / MONDAY
Easter Monday (Orthodox)

14 / TUESDAY

15 / WEDNESDAY

THREE POSITIVE THINGS THIS WEEK

1 _____

2 _____

3 _____

> ## "When the breath is unsteady, all is unsteady; when the breath is still, all is still."

GORAKSHA (c.11–12TH CENTURY), YOGI

16 / THURSDAY

17 / FRIDAY ●

18 / SATURDAY

_____

_____

_____

_____

_____

_____

19 / SUNDAY

_____

_____

_____

_____

_____

JUST BREATHE

It's important to be mindful of our breathing and our bodies. Often, we tense up and alter our breathing without realizing. Stop, relax your jaw, unclench your hands and drop your shoulders. Take a deep breath right down into your stomach and then exhale. Practise mindful breathing whenever you feel rising tension.

APR 20 – APR 26
STILLNESS

20 / MONDAY ♉

21 / TUESDAY

22 / WEDNESDAY
Earth Day

THREE POSITIVE THINGS THIS WEEK

1
2
3

> ## "There is the sense of the desert hills, that there is room enough and time enough."
>
> MARY HUNTER AUSTIN (1868–1934), NATURE WRITER

23 / THURSDAY
St George's Day

24 / FRIDAY ☽

25 / SATURDAY
Anzac Day

26 / SUNDAY

IMMERSE YOURSELF IN NATURE

Nature aids healing and creates a feeling of serenity. This week, find or make your own pocket of nature to enjoy, whether that's by going for a walk in the woods or buying yourself some flowers to display at home. Big or small, nature can be a wonderful way to reconnect with a sense of stillness and peace.

APRIL OVERVIEW

M	TU	W	TH	F	SA	SU
30	31	1	2	3	4	5
6	7	8	9	10	11	12
13	14	15	16	17	18	19
20	21	22	23	24	25	26
27	28	29	30	1	2	3

This month I am grateful for . . .

REFLECTIONS ON STILLNESS

How has stripping back and embracing stillness been beneficial for you this month?

_____

_____

_____

_____

_____

How might you be able to find more moments of stillness in your daily life moving forward?

_____

_____

_____

_____

_____

As you breathe gently, draw a line on a piece of paper that represents your breath, allowing your pen or pencil to move up and down with each inhalation and exhalation. Mindfully soak up the stillness in this simple activity.

MAY

RESTORATION

We've all experienced particular things in the past that have helped to shape us, whether for good or bad. Often, bad experiences can leave a deeper impact than we would like and can start affecting our present, too. Whether something that happened in our childhood, a problem in a previous relationship or just an offhand comment someone once made, certain past events can sometimes influence how we react and deal with moments in our lives here and now.

These emotional wounds from the past can be hard to face, but working on recognizing them and processing them helps. Sometimes, we will be able to easily recognize them and sometimes we won't. Sometimes, it takes a professional to dig deep and help us to find the root cause. Either way, the work is in the emotional healing and the restoration of a healthy sense of self.

This month's prompts aim to help you find gentle ways to rebuild your sense of self and concentrate on finding a way to move forward with self-forgiveness and love.

AFFIRMATION OF THE MONTH

I am worth taking care of

APR 27 – MAY 3
RESTORATION

27 / MONDAY

28 / TUESDAY

29 / WEDNESDAY

THREE POSITIVE THINGS THIS WEEK

1

2

3

> ## "I celebrate myself, and sing myself."
>
> WALT WHITMAN (1819–1892), POET AND ESSAYIST

30 / THURSDAY

1 / FRIDAY ○
Beltane
Vesak Day (Buddha Day)

2 / SATURDAY

3 / SUNDAY

CELEBRATE GETTING THROUGH IT ALL

Every time you've faced a challenge and made your way through a crisis, you've exercised resilience and found a way to restore yourself. Think of a time when you were really struggling and now commend yourself for getting through it – because you deserve to feel proud of that. Let it inspire you next time you face a challenge.

MAY 4 – MAY 10
RESTORATION

4 / MONDAY
Early May Bank Holiday
(UK, ROI)

_____
_____
_____
_____
_____
_____
_____
_____
_____
_____
_____
_____

5 / TUESDAY
Cinco de Mayo

_____
_____
_____
_____
_____
_____
_____
_____
_____
_____
_____
_____

6 / WEDNESDAY

_____
_____
_____
_____
_____
_____
_____
_____
_____
_____
_____
_____

THREE POSITIVE THINGS THIS WEEK

1 _____
2 _____
3 _____

"Dare to declare who you are."

HILDEGARD OF BINGEN (1098–1179), ABBESS AND POLYMATH

7 / THURSDAY

8 / FRIDAY

9 / SATURDAY ☾

10 / SUNDAY
Mother's Day (USA, CAN, AUS, NZ)

RESTORE YOUR FAITH IN YOURSELF

Our internal voices can say the harshest things. This week, try to be aware of the voice inside your head. When it says something negative, reframe this with a positive. For example, "I hate being so sensitive" might become "I'm grateful for how my sensitivity allows me to connect with myself and others on a deeper level".

11 / MONDAY	12 / TUESDAY	13 / WEDNESDAY

THREE POSITIVE THINGS THIS WEEK

1
2
3

> "I am not afraid of storms, for I am learning how to sail my ship."

LOUISA MAY ALCOTT (1832–1888), NOVELIST

14 / THURSDAY
Ascension Day

15 / FRIDAY

16 / SATURDAY ●

17 / SUNDAY

LEARN THAT SELF-CARE ISN'T SELFISH

No matter how resilient we are, we need to remember to take care of ourselves. Self-care restores us and helps us to deal with all that life throws at us, so take some time this week to focus on yourself. Time to replenish your own resources is important – you deserve to give that to yourself.

MAY 18 – MAY 24
RESTORATION

18 / MONDAY
Victoria Day (CAN,
exc NS, NB, QC)

19 / TUESDAY

20 / WEDNESDAY

THREE POSITIVE THINGS THIS WEEK

1
2
3

21 / THURSDAY ♊

22 / FRIDAY

23 / SATURDAY ☽

_____

_____

_____

_____

_____

24 / SUNDAY
Pentecost (Whit Sunday)

_____

_____

_____

LET GO OF PAST HURTS

It's often hard to let go of negative emotions, so the act of writing can help you with this, allowing you to get past hurts out of your system and move on. This week, identify something negative that you're holding on to and write it down. Perhaps even screw it up and throw it away. Then see how you feel.

MAY 25 – MAY 31
RESTORATION

25 / MONDAY
Spring Bank Holiday (UK)
Memorial Day (USA)
Whit Monday

26 / TUESDAY

27 / WEDNESDAY
Eid al-Adha (Feast of the
Sacrifice) begins at sundown

THREE POSITIVE THINGS THIS WEEK

1
2
3

> ## "The more you know yourself, the more you forgive yourself."
>
> CONFUCIUS (551–479 BCE), PHILOSOPHER

28 / THURSDAY

29 / FRIDAY

30 / SATURDAY

31 / SUNDAY ○
Trinity Sunday

FORGIVE YOURSELF

To heal from past mistakes, we need to forgive ourselves. When we no longer feel shame or regret, we open ourselves up to the possibility of restorative healing. Think of something you're struggling to forgive yourself for and use this affirmation: "I'm human and sometimes I make mistakes, but I'm always worthy of forgiveness".

MAY OVERVIEW

M	TU	W	TH	F	SA	SU
27	28	29	30	1	2	3
4	5	6	7	8	9	10
11	12	13	14	15	16	17
18	19	20	21	22	23	24
25	26	27	28	29	30	31

This month I am grateful for . . .

REFLECTIONS ON RESTORATION

How has it felt this month to focus on really looking after yourself, reflecting on past difficulties and starting to restore a healthier sense of self?

_____

_____

_____

_____

_____

Do you think you still have restorative healing to do?

_____

_____

_____

_____

_____

Draw five flowers. In the middle of each one, write something from your past that you forgive yourself for. You deserve to forgive your past, so that you can move more freely into your future.

DREAMS

We all have dreams and aspirations, things we'd love to do or goals we'd love to achieve. This month is about the power of your dreams and imagination. It's about championing the act of letting our minds wander and thinking about what could be.

Not only is dreaming a bit of escapism and fun, it can be a wonderful way to find out what we really want. It can inspire us to do things we wouldn't normally do and push us to take scary leaps into the unknown. Dreaming gives us hope and a sense of possibility. Never underestimate the power of dreaming and where it might lead. So many wonderful things in this world started out as a dream in someone's head.

Use the prompts this month to explore your own hopes and dreams for the future and have some fun imagining where they could lead you.

AFFIRMATION OF THE MONTH

I am making my dreams come true

JUN 1 – JUN 7
DREAMS

1 / MONDAY
Western Australia Day (WA)

2 / TUESDAY

3 / WEDNESDAY

THREE POSITIVE THINGS THIS WEEK

1

2

3

> *"You have within you the strength, the patience, and the passion to reach for the stars to change the world."*
>
> HARRIET TUBMAN (1822–1913), ACTIVIST

4 / THURSDAY
Corpus Christi

5 / FRIDAY

6 / SATURDAY

_____

7 / SUNDAY

IMAGINE YOUR DREAM FUTURE

What would your ideal future look like? Would you like to work less and spend more time with friends and family? Would you like to visit somewhere in particular or take up a new hobby? This week, have a think about how you could potentially make some small changes to put your dreams into action.

JUN 8 – JUN 14
DREAMS

8 / MONDAY ☾	9 / TUESDAY	10 / WEDNESDAY

THREE POSITIVE THINGS THIS WEEK

1
2
3

> *"Dreams are today's answers to tomorrow's questions."*
>
> EDGAR CAYCE (1877–1945), MYSTIC AND AUTHOR

11 / THURSDAY

_____
_____
_____
_____
_____
_____
_____
_____
_____
_____

12 / FRIDAY

_____
_____
_____
_____
_____
_____
_____
_____
_____
_____

13 / SATURDAY

_____
_____
_____

14 / SUNDAY

_____
_____
_____
_____
_____
_____

CREATE A DREAM BOARD

Dream or vision boards are a fun way to create a visual representation of your hopes and goals. Take time out this week to envisage your ideal state of being. Then find images and quotes that fit this vision and use them to create a visually appealing overview – whether on-screen or on paper – of what's most important to you.

JUN 15 – JUN 21
DREAMS

15 / MONDAY ●

_____

_____

_____

_____

_____

_____

_____

_____

_____

_____

_____

_____

16 / TUESDAY

Islamic New Year (first day
of Muharram)

_____

_____

_____

_____

_____

_____

_____

_____

_____

_____

_____

_____

17 / WEDNESDAY

_____

_____

_____

_____

_____

_____

_____

_____

_____

_____

_____

_____

THREE POSITIVE THINGS THIS WEEK

1 _____

2 _____

3 _____

> ## "If you want to do it, you can do it. The question is, do you want to do it?"
>
> NELLIE BLY (1864–1922), INVESTIGATIVE REPORTER

18 / THURSDAY

19 / FRIDAY
Juneteenth (USA)

20 / SATURDAY
King's Birthday

21 / SUNDAY ☽ ♋
Summer Solstice (UK, ROI, USA, CAN)
Father's Day (UK, ROI, USA, CAN)
Winter Solstice (AUS, NZ)

TACKLE YOUR FEARS

Sometimes our dreams are within our reach, but obtaining them feels difficult because of our fears. This week, identify something that's stopping you from reaching a particular dream and try to envisage how you can tackle the problem in order to move forward.

JUN 22 – JUN 28

DREAMS

22 / MONDAY	23 / TUESDAY	24 / WEDNESDAY

THREE POSITIVE THINGS THIS WEEK

1 _____

2 _____

3 _____

"Travelling – it leaves you speechless, then turns you into a storyteller."

IBN BATTUTA (1304–1377), EXPLORER AND SCHOLAR

25 / THURSDAY

_____
_____
_____
_____
_____
_____
_____
_____
_____
_____

26 / FRIDAY

_____
_____
_____
_____
_____
_____
_____
_____
_____
_____

27 / SATURDAY

_____
_____
_____
_____

28 / SUNDAY

_____
_____
_____
_____
_____
_____

CREATE A TRAVEL BUCKET LIST

Is there anywhere that you've dreamed of visiting but have never quite made it? This week, have a think about where those places might be and make a list of them. It could be anywhere at all! Then refer back to this list when you might be in the position to make one of those dream trips a reality.

JUNE OVERVIEW

M	TU	W	TH	F	SA	SU
1	2	3	4	5	6	7
8	9	10	11	12	13	14
15	16	17	18	19	20	21
22	23	24	25	26	27	28
29	30	1	2	3	4	5

This month I am grateful for . . .

_____

_____

_____

_____

_____

_____

_____

_____

_____

REFLECTIONS ON DREAMS

How has it felt this month to reflect on your dreams and what you'd like from life?

_____

_____

_____

_____

_____

Are any of your dreams attainable in the near future?

_____

_____

_____

_____

_____

Complete the sentence "My life is ..." with your biggest and wildest dreams for the future. Then keep this note somewhere as a reminder whenever you need a boost of optimism.

_____

_____

_____

_____

_____

CONNECTION

We all need connection – it's a basic human need, even if we don't always realize it. Sometimes when we feel at our worst, it can be easy to hide ourselves away, but reaching out to someone, forcing ourselves to interact with others or just being around other people can have massive positive benefits for our emotional wellbeing and mental health.

Nothing beats having a belly laugh with a friend, and sometimes all we need is a quick catch-up with a loved one to feel like our cup is a little fuller. We're human; we weren't built to do everything alone. Connection doesn't always have to mean meeting in person. A lovely message from someone dear can really lift your mood, or finding a friend online who is going through something similar to you can offer such a feeling of reassurance.

Use this month's prompts to discover the beauty of connection and see how it could impact your day-to-day life.

AFFIRMATION OF THE MONTH

I am worthy of love
and connection

JUN 29 – JUL 5
CONNECTION

29 / MONDAY ○	30 / TUESDAY	1 / WEDNESDAY
		Canada Day

THREE POSITIVE THINGS THIS WEEK

1
2
3

> ## "Be kind, for everyone you meet is fighting a harder battle."
>
> IAN MACLAREN (1850–1907), MINISTER AND AUTHOR

2 / THURSDAY

_____
_____
_____
_____
_____
_____
_____
_____
_____
_____
_____

3 / FRIDAY

_____
_____
_____
_____
_____
_____
_____
_____
_____
_____
_____

4 / SATURDAY
Independence Day (USA)

_____
_____
_____
_____

5 / SUNDAY

_____
_____
_____
_____
_____

PRACTISE COMPASSIONATE CONNECTION

The world is busy, and emotions can sometimes get the better of us in times of stress. This week, when confronted with somebody else's anger or frustration, try to find the strength to practise more compassion. Does it lead to a shift in the dynamic or a deeper level of connection?

JUL 6 – JUL 12

CONNECTION

6 / MONDAY	7 / TUESDAY ☾	8 / WEDNESDAY

THREE POSITIVE THINGS THIS WEEK

1 _____

2 _____

3 _____

> ## "We have two ears and one mouth, so we should listen more than we say."

ZENO OF CITIUM (c.335–263 BCE), PHILOSOPHER

9 / THURSDAY

_____
_____
_____
_____
_____
_____
_____
_____
_____
_____

10 / FRIDAY

_____
_____
_____
_____
_____
_____
_____
_____
_____
_____

11 / SATURDAY

_____
_____
_____
_____

12 / SUNDAY
Battle of the Boyne (NI)

_____
_____
_____
_____

LISTEN MORE CAREFULLY

Are you a good listener? If yes, what do you think makes you good? If no, how might you improve? Perhaps you need to worry less about what to say next, or give the speaker more space before replying? This week, focus on listening more intently and see whether this helps you to connect with people on a deeper level.

13 / MONDAY
Battle of the Boyne (NI)
observed

14 / TUESDAY ●
Bastille Day

15 / WEDNESDAY

_____

THREE POSITIVE THINGS THIS WEEK

1 _____

2 _____

3 _____

> "The blessing it is to have a friend to whom one can speak fearlessly on any subject."

DINAH CRAIK (1826–1887), WRITER

16 / THURSDAY

17 / FRIDAY

18 / SATURDAY

19 / SUNDAY

ENCOURAGE OTHERS TO OPEN UP

Often when we ask, "How are you?" we leave it at that. What would happen if you followed it up with, "How are you really?" Try that with someone this week and see what happens. Although only a small gesture, it might just create the little bit of extra space and connection they need to open up.

JUL 20 – JUL 26

CONNECTION

20 / MONDAY

21 / TUESDAY ☽

22 / WEDNESDAY ♌

THREE POSITIVE THINGS THIS WEEK

1

2

3

> "The world is round so that friendship may encircle it."

PIERRE TEILHARD DE CHARDIN (1881–1955), POLYMATH

23 / THURSDAY

24 / FRIDAY

25 / SATURDAY

26 / SUNDAY

REACH OUT TO SOMEONE

When life gets busy, time slips by and we may realize we haven't spoken to someone we care about in a while. Is there a loved one that you haven't contacted for some time? Reach out to let them know that they're in your thoughts and that you value their friendship and the feeling of connection that brings.

JULY OVERVIEW

M	TU	W	TH	F	SA	SU
29	30	1	2	3	4	5
6	7	8	9	10	11	12
13	14	15	16	17	18	19
20	21	22	23	24	25	26
27	28	29	30	31	1	2

this month I am grateful for . . .

_____

_____

_____

_____

_____

_____

_____

_____

_____

REFLECTIONS ON CONNECTION

How did it feel to concentrate on connection this month?

_____

_____

_____

_____

_____

_____

In what ways would you like to have more opportunities for connection in your life?

_____

_____

_____

_____

_____

_____

Feeling connected is very grounding. This month, write an old-fashioned note to someone special and let them know you're thinking of them. Post it to them in the knowledge that your small act might just make their day.

EMPOWERMENT

How many times have you let an opportunity slip away because you didn't feel good enough? Or have you ever wished you had the confidence to do something but never quite managed it? Often, we can get stuck in our comfort zones, pulled into cycles of negative talk or caught up in habits that we know aren't good for us. If these things aren't serving us well and actually make us feel worse, perhaps it's time to find new habits and goals – ones that build our confidence, support our emotional and physical wellbeing, and make us feel the best and most fulfilled we can be.

When do you feel at your most empowered? Or is that something you struggle to feel? This month's prompts will help you to explore different ways of empowering yourself and embracing all that makes you brilliant! Empowerment isn't a one-size-fits-all concept, so it's important to find what makes you feel strong, confident and unstoppable.

AFFIRMATION OF THE MONTH

I am strong, capable and brave;
all I need is within me

JUL 27 – AUG 2
EMPOWERMENT

27 / MONDAY

28 / TUESDAY

29 / WEDNESDAY ○

THREE POSITIVE THINGS THIS WEEK

1 _____

2 _____

3 _____

> ## "Never let the fear of striking out keep you from playing the game."
>
> BABE RUTH (1895–1948), BASEBALL PITCHER

30 / THURSDAY

_____
_____
_____
_____
_____
_____
_____
_____
_____
_____
_____
_____

31 / FRIDAY

_____
_____
_____
_____
_____
_____
_____
_____
_____
_____
_____
_____

1 / SATURDAY
Lughnasadh (Lammas)

_____
_____
_____
_____

2 / SUNDAY

_____
_____
_____
_____
_____
_____

WHAT EMPOWERS ME?

Different people tend to find different things empowering. This week, think about what makes you feel more empowered – it can even be small things, like ticking off your to do list or practising self-care. Can implement more of these in your daily life, so you can feel empowered more of the time?

AUG 3 – AUG 9
EMPOWERMENT

3 / MONDAY
Early Summer Bank Holiday
(ROI, SCO)
Public Holiday (NSW, NT)

4 / TUESDAY

5 / WEDNESDAY

THREE POSITIVE THINGS THIS WEEK

1

2

3

> "There is no gate, no lock, no bolt that you can set upon the freedom of my mind."
>
> VIRGINIA WOOLF (1882–1941), WRITER

6 / THURSDAY ☾

7 / FRIDAY

8 / SATURDAY

_____

_____

_____

_____

_____

9 / SUNDAY

_____

_____

_____

_____

BE TRUE TO YOU

Sometimes other people's (or society's) expectations of us can hold us back from feeling fully empowered. This week, write a list of how you feel pigeonholed or limited by others' views of you. Could you implement any small changes to break free from these limiting generalizations?

AUG 10 – AUG 16
EMPOWERMENT

10 / MONDAY

11 / TUESDAY

12 / WEDNESDAY ⬤

THREE POSITIVE THINGS THIS WEEK

1

2

3

> ## "I attribute my success to this: I never gave or took any excuse."
>
> FLORENCE NIGHTINGALE (1820–1910), SOCIAL REFORMER

13 / THURSDAY

14 / FRIDAY

15 / SATURDAY

_____
_____
_____
_____
_____

16 / SUNDAY

_____
_____
_____
_____
_____

WHEN DID YOU LAST FEEL EMPOWERED?

Think back over your life and pinpoint when you last felt most empowered. Where were you? What were you doing? Next time you feel small, undervalued or insignificant, think back to that occasion and remind yourself of how amazing, strong and capable you are.

AUG 17 – AUG 23
EMPOWERMENT

17 / MONDAY

18 / TUESDAY

19 / WEDNESDAY

THREE POSITIVE THINGS THIS WEEK

1
2
3

> ## "You can control any situation if you first control yourself."

FLORENCE SCOVEL SHINN (1871–1940), AUTHOR AND ILLUSTRATOR

20 / THURSDAY ☽

21 / FRIDAY

22 / SATURDAY

23 / SUNDAY ♍

GIVE YOURSELF A PEP TALK

Sometimes all we need is a good pep talk to make us feel more empowered again. This week, turn to the Inspired Journalling section at the back of this diary and write your own pep talk for use in times of need. Try to write as many positive, inspiring and empowering things as you can so it helps you in your next low moment.

AUG 24 – AUG 30
EMPOWERMENT

24 / MONDAY

25 / TUESDAY
Milad un-Nabi (birth of the Prophet Muhammed)

26 / WEDNESDAY

THREE POSITIVE THINGS THIS WEEK

1
2
3

> "The most difficult thing is the decision to act. The rest is merely tenacity."

AMELIA EARHART (1897–c.1937), AVIATOR

27 / THURSDAY

28 / FRIDAY ○

29 / SATURDAY

30 / SUNDAY

STEP OUT OF YOUR COMFORT ZONE

Have you ever wanted to join a group but found yourself a little nervous to take the first step? This week, gently try to push yourself to finally do it. Whether it's an in-person meet-up or an online group of likeminded people, see how biting the bullet and doing something you've been wanting to do for ages makes you feel.

AUGUST OVERVIEW

M	TU	W	TH	F	SA	SU
27	28	29	30	31	1	2
3	4	5	6	7	8	9
10	11	12	13	14	15	16
17	18	19	20	21	22	23
24	25	26	27	28	29	30
31	1	2	3	4	5	6

This month I am grateful for . . .

_____
_____
_____
_____
_____
_____
_____

REFLECTIONS ON EMPOWERMENT

How did it feel to concentrate on your feelings of empowerment this month?

_____

_____

_____

_____

_____

_____

In what ways would you like to add more empowering things into your life?
How can you implement this?

_____

_____

_____

_____

_____

_____

Find a picture of yourself that you like and print it off. Write down everything you love about yourself on this – your skills, your strengths and all the rest. Whenever you need an empowering boost, look at it to remind yourself that you're amazing!

SEPTEMBER

SELF-SOOTHING

How do you soothe yourself in your most difficult times? What makes you feel better or comforted? Born without the ability to self-regulate, at first we rely on our caregivers to be our calm, safe place. Being able to soothe ourselves is something we learn gradually, yet as adults we can often forget how important it is to do this.

Finding small, healthy ways to cope with life's big emotions is a skill that we can draw on again and again. Whether it's participating in something crafty, making something with our hands or writing our feelings in a journal, there are plenty of healthy ways to self-soothe. Perhaps for you it's going for a walk in the fresh air or relaxing in a deep, warm bath. Whatever it is, knowing how we can be our own best advocates in times of trouble is a wonderful thing.

So use this month's prompts to investigate what supports and soothes you.

AFFIRMATION OF THE MONTH

I am safe, I am loved,
I will be okay

AUG 31 – SEP 6

SELF-SOOTHING

31 / MONDAY
Late Summer Bank Holiday
(UK exc SCO)

1 / TUESDAY

2 / WEDNESDAY

THREE POSITIVE THINGS THIS WEEK

1
2
3

> ## "Deliberately seek opportunities for kindness, sympathy and patience."

EVELYN UNDERHILL (1875–1941), WRITER

3 / THURSDAY

_____
_____
_____
_____
_____
_____
_____
_____
_____

_____

4 / FRIDAY ☾

_____
_____
_____
_____
_____
_____
_____
_____
_____

_____

5 / SATURDAY

_____
_____
_____
_____

6 / SUNDAY
Father's Day (AUS, NZ)

_____
_____
.
_____

_____

IDENTIFY WHAT SOOTHES YOU

It's important to know what soothes us in our most difficult times, as this gives us the tools to help ourselves and cradle ourselves in our darkest moments. This week, turn to the Inspired Journalling section at the back of this diary and make a list of all the things you find soothing when the going gets tough.

SEP 7 – SEP 13
SELF-SOOTHING

7 / MONDAY
Labor Day (USA, CAN)

8 / TUESDAY

9 / WEDNESDAY

THREE POSITIVE THINGS THIS WEEK

1
2
3

> ## "Where words fail, music speaks."
> HANS CHRISTIAN ANDERSEN (1805–1875), AUTHOR

10 / THURSDAY

11 / FRIDAY ●
Rosh Hashanah (Jewish New Year) begins at sundown

12 / SATURDAY

13 / SUNDAY

CREATE A SOOTHING PLAYLIST

Music can be a wonderful source of comfort in difficult or stressful moments. Spend some time this week creating a playlist of all your favourite soothing songs that bring you a serene feeling. Anytime you need a little peaceful grounding, put on your headphones and soak up the soothing vibes.

14 / MONDAY

15 / TUESDAY

16 / WEDNESDAY

THREE POSITIVE THINGS THIS WEEK

1

2

3

> ## "Clouds come floating into my life, no longer to carry rain or usher storm, but to add colour to my sunset sky."

RABINDRANATH TAGORE (1861–1941), POET AND COMPOSER

17 / THURSDAY

18 / FRIDAY ☽

19 / SATURDAY

20 / SUNDAY

Yom Kippur (Day of
Atonement) begins
at sundown

WATCH THE CLOUDS DRIFT BY

Overthinking things can prevent us from finding
a place of soothing inner calm. If you're an over-
thinker, try to imagine your whirling thoughts
as being like the weather. Allow each thought
to be like a cloud floating past. Acknowledge
it's there, but know that it cannot be changed
or turned into anything other than it is.

SEP 21 – SEP 27
SELF-SOOTHING

21 / MONDAY
International Day of Peace

22 / TUESDAY

23 / WEDNESDAY ♎
Autumn Equinox (UK, ROI, USA, CAN)
Spring Equinox (AUS, NZ)

THREE POSITIVE THINGS THIS WEEK

1

2

3

> ## "The words of kindness are more healing to a drooping heart than balm or honey."

SARAH FIELDING (1710–1768), AUTHOR

24 / THURSDAY

25 / FRIDAY
Sukkot (Feast of the Tabernacles) begins at sundown

26 / SATURDAY ○

27 / SUNDAY

COMPILE WORDS OF COMFORT

Words can hold so much power. Take a moment this week to write down some soothing words of comfort for yourself and stick them in a place where you will see them often, such as on the fridge or bathroom mirror. Whether a favourite lyric, quote or homemade affirmation, let these words be there for you when you need them.

SEPTEMBER OVERVIEW

M	TU	W	TH	F	SA	SU
31	1	2	3	4	5	6
7	8	9	10	11	12	13
14	15	16	17	18	19	20
21	22	23	24	25	26	27
28	29	30	1	2	3	4

This month I am grateful for . . .

REFLECTIONS ON SELF-SOOTHING

How have you made more time for soothing yourself this month?

_____

_____

_____

_____

_____

Has practising self-soothing had an impact on how you feel?

_____

_____

_____

_____

_____

Both soothe your soul and ground yourself by doing some scribbling on a piece of paper. Then mindfully colour in all the shapes that the scribbles have made and/or the gaps between them.

OCTOBER

BALANCE

Balance is such an integral and important aspect of life. To take good care of ourselves, it's good to aim for balance in all aspects of our daily lives. When we feel balanced we work better, we improve our relationships, we have increased focus and we generally have better emotional and physical wellbeing.

Of course, achieving balance is often easier said than done, and it tends to be an ongoing learning process. Life is neither easy nor straightforward, and sometimes the scales tip more in one direction than the other, meaning that we risk neglecting different areas of our lives. The important thing is that we recognize when this is happening and take the steps needed to find a sense of stability again.

This month, use the weekly prompts to help you find and implement more balance in your life.

AFFIRMATION OF THE MONTH

Every day, I make the time to work on all of my goals equally

SEP 28 – OCT 4
BALANCE

28 / MONDAY	29 / TUESDAY	30 / WEDNESDAY

THREE POSITIVE THINGS THIS WEEK

1 _____
2 _____
3 _____

> "What I dream of is an art of balance."

HENRI MATISSE (1869–1954), PAINTER

1 / THURSDAY
Black History Month
begins (UK)

2 / FRIDAY
Sukkot ends at sundown
Shemini Atzeret begins
at sundown

3 / SATURDAY ☾
Simchat Torah begins
at sundown

4 / SUNDAY

EVALUATE THE BALANCE IN YOUR LIFE

Life will always have its ups and downs and
stressful moments. This week, look at the
current causes of imbalance and stress in your
life. Ask yourself, "What things would need
to be removed from my life for me to feel
more balanced and still? Could I change or say
goodbye to at least some of these things?"

BALANCE

5 / MONDAY

_____
_____
_____
_____
_____
_____
_____
_____
_____
_____
_____
_____
_____

6 / TUESDAY

_____
_____
_____
_____
_____
_____
_____
_____
_____
_____
_____
_____
_____

7 / WEDNESDAY

_____
_____
_____
_____
_____
_____
_____
_____
_____
_____
_____
_____
_____

THREE POSITIVE THINGS THIS WEEK

1 _____
2 _____
3 _____

> "The oldest, shortest words – 'yes' and 'no' – are those that require most thought."

PYTHAGORAS (*c.*570–*c.*495 BCE), PHILOSOPHER AND MATHEMATICIAN

8 / THURSDAY

9 / FRIDAY

10 / SATURDAY ●

11 / SUNDAY

REMEMBER IT'S OKAY TO SAY NO

It can be hard to say "no" without feeling like we're letting people down or they'll be annoyed with us, and sometimes we say "yes" when we know we shouldn't. Next time someone asks you to do something, remind yourself that it's okay to say no. Occasionally, we may need to say no so we can regain some personal balance.

OCT 12 – OCT 18
BALANCE

12 / MONDAY
Indigenous Peoples' Day/
Columbus Day (USA)
Thanksgiving (CAN)

13 / TUESDAY

14 / WEDNESDAY

THREE POSITIVE THINGS THIS WEEK

1
2
3

> "Life is like riding a bicycle. To keep your balance you must keep moving."

ALBERT EINSTEIN(1879-1955), THEORETICAL PHYSICIST

15 / THURSDAY

16 / FRIDAY

17 / SATURDAY

18 / SUNDAY ☽

FIND YOUR MOST BALANCED SELF

This week, think about when you're your best self, at your most happy and balanced. Is this a strong feeling? Does it happen often? And what helps to bring it on? When you've answered these questions, look at how you can bring this feeling more often in your life and hopefully feel more balanced going forward.

OCT 19 – OCT 25
BALANCE

19 / MONDAY	20 / TUESDAY	21 / WEDNESDAY

THREE POSITIVE THINGS THIS WEEK

1
2
3

> *"Freedom so often means that one isn't needed anywhere."*
>
> WILLA CATHER (1873–1947), NOVELIST

22 / THURSDAY

23 / FRIDAY ♏

24 / SATURDAY

25 / SUNDAY

British Summer Time ends
Daylight Saving Time ends
(UK)

SET SOME DIGITAL BOUNDARIES

In our busy lives, balance can be difficult to achieve due to the 24/7 pull of online life. This week, think about boundaries you could put in place to tackle that. You could limit time spent on certain apps, mute phone notifications or restrict work emails to your computer only. See if this makes a difference to your inner balance.

OCTOBER OVERVIEW

M	TU	W	TH	F	SA	SU
28	29	30	1	2	3	4
5	6	7	8	9	10	11
12	13	14	15	16	17	18
19	20	21	22	23	24	25
26	27	28	29	30	31	1

this month I am grateful for . . .

REFLECTIONS ON BALANCE

How have you found focusing on balance within your life this month?

_____

_____

_____

_____

_____

In what ways do you think finding a better balance could help you?

_____

_____

_____

_____

_____

Sometimes, letting things go can help to restore balance in our lives. Get a piece of paper and draw around both your hands. On one, write down the tasks that are currently essential. On the other, write down anything you can let go of. Does this help you feel a little more balanced?

don't miss out on next year's diary! see the back page for details on how to order your copy

ADAPTABILITY

How easy do you find it to be flexible and embrace change in your life? Is change something you accept or do you find yourself pushing against it?

Being able to relax, go with the flow and adapt to change comes more easily to some than others. While there are those who seem to take it all in their stride, for others it can feel much trickier. Although there's nothing wrong with finding it tricky, this approach can end up being quite limiting and holding us back in the long term.

Change challenges us but it also gives us the opportunity to learn, to be creative, to problem-solve and to find excitement in the unknown. As long as we honour our feelings and listen to ourselves and what we're comfortable with, pushing ourselves to be a little more adaptable can be incredibly freeing and lead us to things we'd never considered doable or possible before.

AFFIRMATION OF THE MONTH

I can confidently adapt and overcome any obstacle

OCT 26 – NOV 1
ADAPTABILITY

26 / MONDAY ○
Labour Day (NZ)
October Bank Holiday (ROI)

27 / TUESDAY

28 / WEDNESDAY

THREE POSITIVE THINGS THIS WEEK

1
2
3

> ## "Adapt or perish, now as ever, is nature's inexorable imperative."
>
> H G WELLS (1866–1946), WRITER

29 / THURSDAY

30 / FRIDAY

31 / SATURDAY
Halloween
Samhain

1 / SUNDAY ☾
All Saints' Day
Daylight Saving Time ends
(USA, CAN)

CAN YOU ADAPT TO CHANGE?

Our comfort levels about adapting to change can differ considerably from person to person. Some people embrace it, while others find it much harder to adjust to. Have a think about how you responded to the most recent change that came into your life. Did you find it difficult? If so, ask yourself why this might be.

NOV 2 – NOV 8
ADAPTABILITY

2 / MONDAY
All Souls' Day

3 / TUESDAY

4 / WEDNESDAY

THREE POSITIVE THINGS THIS WEEK

1 _____

2 _____

3 _____

> ## "Nothing is so painful to the human mind as a great and sudden change."
>
> MARY SHELLEY (1797–1851), NOVELIST

5 / THURSDAY
Guy Fawkes Night

_____
_____
_____
_____
_____
_____
_____
_____
_____
_____

6 / FRIDAY

_____
_____
_____
_____
_____
_____
_____
_____
_____
_____

7 / SATURDAY

_____
_____
_____
_____

8 / SUNDAY
Diwali/Deepavali

_____
_____
_____
_____
_____

REFLECT ON PAST GROWTH

Emotional growth can't happen if we don't learn to adapt to change. So every time something unexpected happens, we have a chance to learn from it and grow. Think about who you were ten years ago: in what ways have you changed since then? Are these changes positive? And what do you think was the catalyst for them?

NOV 9 – NOV 15
ADAPTABILITY

9 / MONDAY ●

10 / TUESDAY

11 / WEDNESDAY

Remembrance Day
(UK, CAN)
Veterans' Day (USA)

THREE POSITIVE THINGS THIS WEEK

1

2

3

> "Happy he who learns to bear what he cannot change."
>
> FRIEDRICH SCHILLER (1759–1805), WRITER

12 / THURSDAY

13 / FRIDAY

14 / SATURDAY

15 / SUNDAY

FOCUS ON WHAT YOU CAN CONTROL

We might find adapting to change difficult when things feel out of our control. However, the reality is we're unable to control everything in life and we'll never feel at peace unless we accept that. This week, try repeating this affirmation: "I concentrate on what I can control and I release everything that I can't."

NOV 16 – NOV 22
ADAPTABILITY

16 / MONDAY	17 / TUESDAY ☽	18 / WEDNESDAY

THREE POSITIVE THINGS THIS WEEK

1
2
3

"Little by little does the trick."

AESOP (c.620–564 BCE), FABULIST

19 / THURSDAY

20 / FRIDAY

21 / SATURDAY
World Hello Day

22 / SUNDAY ♐

APPRECIATE EVEN THE TINY STEPS

Once we've fallen into comfortable routines, adapting to new ones can feel scary. It's okay to take things slowly – step by step. This week, think about something you are struggling to adapt to: are there small steps you can take to make it feel a little easier? Even tiny steps are still steps – and they all add up!

NOV 23– NOV 29
ADAPTABILITY

23 / MONDAY	24 / TUESDAY ○	25 / WEDNESDAY

THREE POSITIVE THINGS THIS WEEK

1
2
3

> ## "The strongest will is the will that knows how to bend."
>
> ALICE DUER MILLER (1874–1942), WRITER

26 / THURSDAY
Thanksgiving Day (USA)

_____
_____
_____
_____
_____
_____
_____
_____
_____
_____

27 / FRIDAY
Black Friday

_____
_____
_____
_____
_____
_____
_____
_____
_____
_____

28 / SATURDAY

_____
_____
_____
_____

29 / SUNDAY
First Sunday of Advent

_____
_____
_____
_____
_____

FIND THE POSITIVES

Sometimes we get hit with a change we didn't expect or want. Think about a change that happened to you that wasn't your immediate choice. How did you find adapting to it? Where did this change lead you? Are you at peace with it now? And did it teach you some lessons or aid your personal growth in any way?

NOVEMBER OVERVIEW

M	TU	W	TH	F	SA	SU
26	27	28	29	30	31	1
2	3	4	5	6	7	8
9	10	11	12	13	14	15
16	17	18	19	20	21	22
23	24	25	26	27	28	29
30	1	2	3	4	5	6

This month I am grateful for . . .

REFLECTIONS ON ADAPTABILITY

How has it felt to focus on adaptability this month?

_____

_____

_____

_____

_____

How have you coped with any moments where being adaptable has been needed?

_____

_____

_____

_____

_____

Draw some blobs using a coloured pen or pencil. Then turn each of the blobs into something – an animal, a flower, a self-portrait, anything. Reflect on how change is inevitable and how our ability to adapt is such a key part of our journey through life.

DECEMBER

REMINISCENCE

Welcome to December, the perfect month in which to reminisce on all that's passed, all we've got through and all we've overcome in the last year!

Reminiscing can bring a sense of sadness sometimes, as we look back over all that's gone – and that's okay. Not all our memories are going to bring us joy or be regarded fondly, but sometimes we can still find lessons in them.

Life is full of ups and downs, and taking some time to look back and reflect can help us to process it and learn from it. Sometimes we can be prompted to find gratitude and, more often than not, we can see with clarity the growth that has been happening all along.

Perhaps there are things we feel we didn't do quite right. Maybe there are things we wish we could get a chance to do again. By taking the time to reminisce, we can offer ourselves the opportunity to move forward with more knowledge and a more compassionate heart.

AFFIRMATION OF THE MONTH

My past does not define my future; I have that choice

NOV 30 – DEC 6
REMINISCENCE

30 / MONDAY
St Andrew's Day (SCO)
Cyber Monday

1 / TUESDAY ☾
World AIDS Day

2 / WEDNESDAY

THREE POSITIVE THINGS THIS WEEK

1
2
3

> "The human mind always makes progress,
> but it is a progress made in spirals."

MADAME DE STAËL (1766–1817), PHILOSOPHER AND POLITICAL THEORIST

3 / THURSDAY

4 / FRIDAY
Hanukkah begins at sundown

5 / SATURDAY

6 / SUNDAY

WRITE A LETTER TO YOUR PAST SELF

How many times have you looked back and wished you'd known then what you know now? Wished you'd known that you would get through it and things would be okay again? This week, turn to the Inspired Journalling section at the back of your diary and write a letter of support to a past you in one of those moments.

DEC 7 – DEC 13
REMINISCENCE

7 / MONDAY

8 / TUESDAY

9 / WEDNESDAY ⬤

THREE POSITIVE THINGS THIS WEEK

1
2
3

> "Every day is a journey, and the journey itself is home."

MATSUO BASHŌ (1644–1694), POET

10 / THURSDAY

11 / FRIDAY

12 / SATURDAY
Hanukkah ends at sundown

13 / SUNDAY

REFLECT ON A PAST DECISION

This week, think about a choice you made this year that you still think about, or maybe even regret. How did making that choice impact you? What do you think you've learned from it? Has it impacted any of the choices you've made since then? If the same situation happened next year, what would you do differently?

DEC 14 – DEC 20
REMINISCENCE

14 / MONDAY	15 / TUESDAY	16 / WEDNESDAY

THREE POSITIVE THINGS THIS WEEK

1 _____

2 _____

3 _____

> "The past, the present and the future are really one: they are today."

HARRIET BEECHER STOWE (1811–1896), AUTHOR AND ABOLITIONIST

17 / THURSDAY ☽

_____
_____
_____
_____
_____
_____
_____
_____
_____
_____
_____

18 / FRIDAY

_____
_____
_____
_____
_____
_____
_____
_____
_____
_____
_____

19 / SATURDAY

_____
_____
_____
_____

20 / SUNDAY

_____
_____
_____
_____
_____

SAY THANK YOU TO 2026!

We often focus on the negatives and dwell on the should-haves, rather than acknowledge and embrace all the wonderful things we've been lucky enough to experience. Reflect on this past year and write down your five favourite things that happened. If five isn't enough, keep going and soak in those glorious memories.

DEC 21 – DEC 27
REMINISCENCE

21 / MONDAY ♑
Winter Solstice (UK, ROI, USA, CAN)

22 / TUESDAY
Summer Solstice (AUS, NZ)

23 / WEDNESDAY

THREE POSITIVE THINGS THIS WEEK

1

2

3

> "The richness of life lies in memories we have forgotten."

CESARE PAVESE (1908–1950), WRITER

24 / THURSDAY ○
Christmas Eve

_____
_____
_____
_____
_____
_____
_____
_____
_____
_____
_____

25 / FRIDAY
Christmas Day

_____
_____
_____
_____
_____
_____
_____
_____
_____
_____
_____

26 / SATURDAY
Boxing Day
Kwanzaa begins

_____
_____
_____
_____

27 / SUNDAY

_____
_____
_____
_____
_____
_____

CREATE A YEARBOOK

This week, have some fun gathering all the photos and mementos from the experiences that made 2026 great and collate them in an album, either manually or digitally. Now, when you want to look back on this particular year, you'll have a specific place to go to remember it.

DEC 28 – JAN 3
REMINISCENCE

28 / MONDAY

29 / TUESDAY

30 / WEDNESDAY ☾

THREE POSITIVE THINGS THIS WEEK

1

2

3

> "If we don't change, we don't grow.
> If we don't grow, we aren't really living."

ANATOLE FRANCE (1844–1924), POET

31 / THURSDAY
New Year's Eve

1 / FRIDAY
New Year's Day
Kwanzaa ends

2 / SATURDAY

3 / SUNDAY

LEARN FROM THE PAST

Sometimes it can be exciting to learn from the past and use those lessons to project ourselves into our future. Think about your goals for next year. What would you like to do? What would you like more of? Is there anything you'd like to let go of? Now's the time to plan and start making those changes.

DECEMBER OVERVIEW

M	TU	W	TH	F	SA	SU
30	1	2	3	4	5	6
7	8	9	10	11	12	13
14	15	16	17	18	19	20
21	22	23	24	25	26	27
28	29	30	31	1	2	3

This month I am grateful for . . .

_____

_____

_____

_____

_____

_____

_____

_____

REFLECTIONS ON REMINISCENCE

How have you found focusing on the theme of reminiscence this month?

_____

_____

_____

_____

_____

Do you feel you could benefit from more reminiscing as you move into 2027?

_____

_____

_____

_____

_____

Draw a butterfly. On one wing, write down your challenges this year. On the other, write down positive outcomes from these. Reflecting on, recognizing and reframing the past can be such a positive tool for personal growth.

INSPIRED JOURNALLING

LET'S GET JOURNALLING

The six journalling pages that follow are a safe space in which you can reflect on different things that will help to make this year as nurturing, empowering and joyful as possible for you. They fit the monthly themes in this diary and are designed to give you room in which to create your own lists and notes – of what you love about life, qualities you like about yourself, your sources of happiness, words of encouragement, reminders of what soothes you and a letter of celebration and support for any challenges you may face in the future

Fill these spaces by writing down your thoughts on each topic. You might find yourself revisiting these at different times and adding to them as you think of new, useful ideas.

Things That I Love in My Life

INTENTION (JANUARY)

What better way to start the year than by reflecting on the things that you love about your life right now? This is a wonderfully grounding activity and the perfect way to gain some clarity about what will be important to you in the months ahead. Honing in on what enhances our lives and fills us up emotionally can make us more aware of what we need to include in our lives going forward.

Use the space below to compile a list of all the things you're grateful for. What makes you feel happy, whole and contented? What makes you feel fulfilled? What gives you purpose? Refer back to this list whenever you need reminding of where to set your intentions this year.

what do I Like About me?

SELF-WORTH (FEBRUARY)

We can be our own worst enemy at times, speaking to ourselves in ways we wouldn't dream of speaking to another person and berating ourselves for not doing better. This constant stream of negativity can affect us more than we think, so it's important to try to become aware of when we're doing it. Recognizing it allows us to steer our minds gently toward a more positive internal voice, which can help shift our negative thought patterns.

Today, take a moment to think about what you love about yourself – anything at all, nothing is too small. It may feel difficult or uncomfortable, but remember there's no judgement here. Just you giving yourself the praise you deserve. Keep this list and refer to it when your self-worth needs a boost.

what Lights me up?

HAPPINESS (MARCH)

Spending time identifying what lights us up and getting to know what makes us happy can help us to perfect where to place our priorities and energy. It will also help us to understand what it's best to seek out when times are tough, based on what will fill us up with the most goodness. By making more time for these key activities, people and places, we can create a happier life for ourselves right now.

With this in mind, write a list of the things that bring you joy – the activites, people and places that make you feel whole, seen, heard and happy; that bring out the best in you. When you're lost or struggling to find your way, use the list to remind yourself of what you might need to make more room for in order to let happiness back in.

write a pep talk for down days

EMPOWERMENT (AUGUST)

We humans can be our own harshest critics. Battling our never-ending worries, perceived failures and internal negative voices can leave us feeling drained and without much confidence in ourselves at all. One way to challenge such negative thought patterns is by writing positive, empowering words about ourselves.

Use the space below to write yourself a little pep talk. There's no need to be self-deprecating here. This is the place to sing your own praises. What makes you the fantastic person you are? What have you done that highlights your best qualities? Write it all down as a reminder that you can turn to when you're next having a tough day and need to feel more empowered.

Things that soothe me

SELF-SOOTHING (SEPTEMBER)

Knowing – and therefore being able to tap into – what we find soothing in times of stress can really help us to maintain and develop our emotional wellbeing. That's why taking the time to get familiar with healthy coping mechanisms is such a valuable thing to do.

So, when you need to self-soothe, do you know what works for you? Use this space to write down anything that you feel could help you in times of difficulty – a "Self-Soothing Tool Kit", if you like. This could include anything from taking a walk, watching TV, crafting or reading, to enjoying a nice warm bath, calling a loved one, having a duvet day or getting an early night. Refer back to this list any time you need some soothing ideas.

Letter to my past self

REMINISCENCE (DECEMBER)

Life is full of ups and downs, trials and tribulations. Along with the wonderful moments come the not-so-great ones. These more challenging times may feel near impossible to get through at times, but we can draw on memories of our strength and resilience in the past to get through.

With this in mind, think back to a difficult time that tested you this year. Write yourself a letter of support. What did you need to hear back then? What message of support can you offer now? Not only will this remind you how resilient and strong you are, but it's a wonderful piece of writing to have in case you hit more turbulent times again. As such, it can not only act as a reassuring letter to your past self but also as a potential letter of support to a future you.

Notes From the Author

Hello, I'm Jess – a designer, illustrator and writer based in South Yorkshire, UK. I run my Instagram page @jessrachelsharp, where I share gentle, positive reminders for when you might need them most. I also have my own line of stationery, enamel pins and gifts, which I sell from my website: www.jessrachelsharp.com. My hope is that my products can offer some support and encouragement through life's many ups and downs.

I began doing what I do after going through a bit of a tough time and attending therapy. I wanted to remember all the helpful words that I was hearing and the life-enhancing epiphanies that I was having, so I began to incorporate them into designs. I started posting them to my Instagram and I realized that not only were they helpful for me, but they resonated with others, too. And I haven't stopped since!

It has been an absolute dream to work with Watkins Publishing on putting these ideas into this diary. I hope you find it as uplifting and inspiring to read and use as I have found it to create.

We are constantly learning and growing on our journey through life, so I hope that this diary can offer some gentle guidance for you along the way – helping you to discover more about yourself and make the very most of each and every day. Here's wishing you much love, hope and happiness for a fulfilling year ahead!

Jess xxx

Notes

Don't miss out on next year's diary!

To pre-order your 2027 *Every Day Matters Diary*
with FREE postage and packing,*
call our UK distributor on +44 (0)1206 255800.

*Free postage and packing for UK delivery addresses only. Offer limited to three books per order.

01 14

WATKINS
Sharing Wisdom
Since 1893

Our books celebrate conscious, passionate, wise and happy living.
Be part of the community by visiting
watkinspublishing.com

f WatkinsPublishing   X @watkinswisdom
▶ WatkinsPublishingLtd   g+ +watkinspublishing1893